Ripley's Believe It or Not!

Developed and produced by Ripley Publishing Ltd

This edition published and distributed by:

Mason Crest
370 Reed Road, Broomall, Pennsylvania 19008
www.masoncrest.com

Printed and bound in the United States of America.

First printing
9 8 7 6 5 4 3 2 1

Ripley's Believe It or Not!
Artistic License
ISBN-13: 978-1-4222-2561-5 (hardcover)
ISBN-13: 978-1-4222-9236-5 (e-book)
Ripley's Believe It or Not!—Complete 16 Title Series
ISBN-13: 978-1-4222-2560-8

Library of Congress Cataloging-in-Publication Data

Artistic license.
    pages cm — (Ripley's believe it or not!)
  ISBN 978-1-4222-2561-5 (hardcover) — ISBN 978-1-4222-2560-8 (series hardcover) —
ISBN 978-1-4222-9236-5 (ebook)
  1. Arts—Miscellanea—Juvenile literature. 2. Curiosities and wonders—Juvenile
literature. I. Title: Artistic license.
  NX67.S44 2012
  700—dc23
                            2012019869

PUBLISHER'S NOTE
While every effort has been made to verify the accuracy of the entries in this book, the Publisher's cannot be held responsible for any errors contained in the work. They would be glad to receive any information from readers.

WARNING
Some of the stunts and activities in this book are undertaken by experts and should not be attempted by anyone without adequate training and supervision.

Disbelief and Shock!

ARTISTIC LICENSE

www.MasonCrest.com

ARTISTIC LICENSE

Breaking the mold. You will never see

such a dazzling display of designs. Open up

to find portraits made out of bar codes, miniature

sculptures made for fleas, and amazing book

carvings created using surgeon's tools.

Artist Jason Hackenwerth creates mystical
creatures using only balloons.

LIGHT SPEED GRAFFITI

A group of German graffiti artists have moved away from daubing walls with spray paint to create dazzling shapes caught on camera, lighting up gloomy cities with energized glowing art. The momentary swirls of light give life to trash cans and create eerie figures on dark streets before dying away into the night.

Based in Cologne, "Lichtfaktor" comprises the graffiti artists Tim Fehske, and David Lupschen and video engineer Marcel Panne. Despite the hi-tech-looking result, the images are made using regular flashlights, neon tubes, glow sticks, LED light, sparklers, and fireworks. The images are "sketched" rapidly by Tim and David, who wear dark clothing so they can hardly be seen in the final product and move quickly out of shot to avoid disrupting the lights. The group then take pictures, using cameras set to an unusually long exposure—10 to 30 seconds—that allows more light to be captured.

The group also makes videos using stop-motion technique, piecing together one light drawing after another to create radiant shapes that come alive on the streets. Their approach to their art is experimental, retaking shots until they get what they want, and they are never sure how the finished pictures will look.

How do you make your pictures?

All our pictures are created with a camera (in one shot). We have a collection of flashlights, biking lights, and flashing LED lights that all work with batteries so that we are completely mobile. We also get good results using fireworks and torches. We like the contrast between the different light sources—for example, xenon gives a golden look and LEDs produce thin, precise lines. We put glasses and other things on the flashlights to get different shapes and colors, or use multi-LED lights and color filters. We like to integrate the surrounding into the picture, for example the trash can (Star Wars vs. Star Trek; far right), which we think is much more interesting than just creating effects in the air. Most of the time we know what we want to draw before we go out, but we are always inspired by our surroundings. And because it's a live process, it's always improvised because you can't plan everything before you actually take the pictures. To get the best results, we use a tripod with an exposure of around 10 to 30 seconds, or longer if needed.

RIPLEY'S ASK

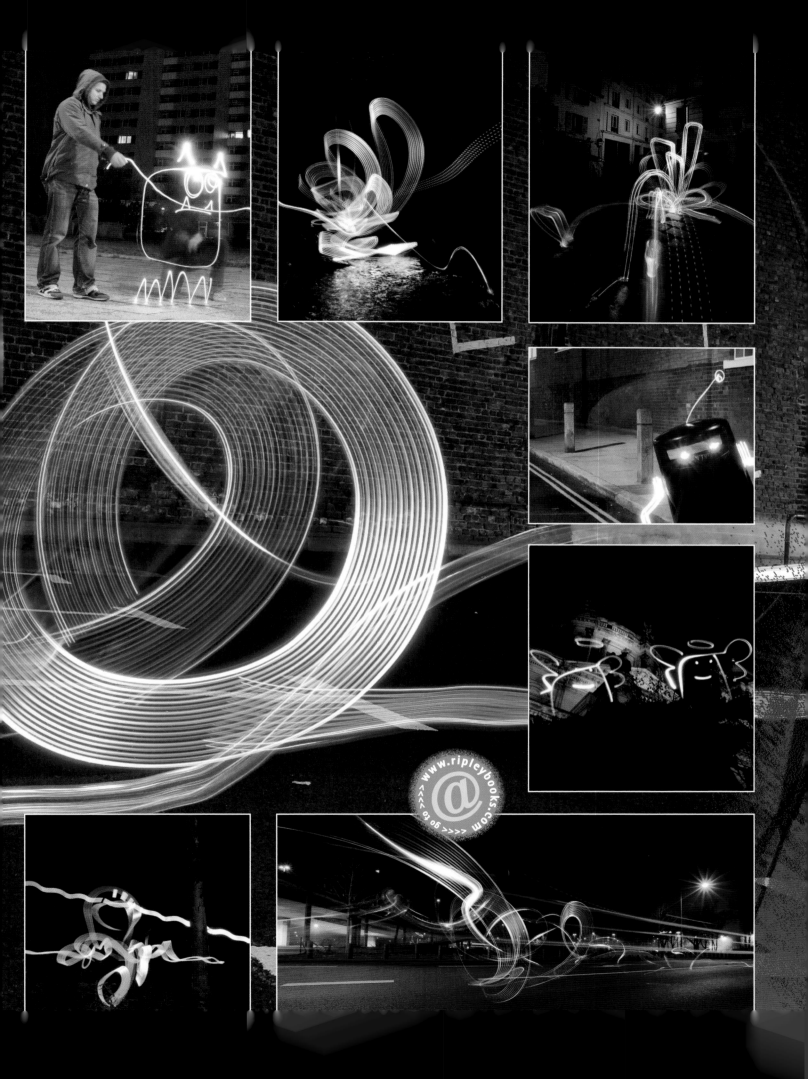

It was painstaking work to complete every hair on each of Bluey's eight legs.

Elizabeth Thompson adds yet more putty to her detailed replica spider.

Arachnid Art

British artist Elizabeth Thompson is seen through the legs of a giant spider that she made from blue putty for a display at England's London Zoo in 2007. The creature was made from 4,000 packs of the putty, measures 4 ft (1.2 m) in width and weighs more than 440 lb (200 kg)—as much as three people. Nicknamed "Bluey," the sculpture is a much larger, and scarier, version of the common house spider.

BLIND PHOTOGRAPHER ■ Alison Bartlett takes amazing photographs of wildlife—even though she has been blind for more than 16 years. Alison, from Hampshire, England, "sees" with her ears, listening for sounds such as rustling in the grass, a bird's wings flapping, or a squirrel nibbling. Her assistant points her in the right direction and gives distances, but the art is all hers. She says: "Of course others have to tell me whether the pictures are any good."

POETIC JUSTICE ■ In December 2007, a large group of teenagers from Vermont were prosecuted for vandalizing the former home of U.S. poet Robert Frost (1874–1963), and their sentencing included classes to learn about Frost's poetry.

GUMMY BEAR ■ Artist Maurizio Savini from Rome, Italy, creates intricate sculptures, which have included a life-size buffalo and a grizzly bear, from thousands of pieces of chewed bubblegum. Maurizio works the gum when it is still warm and manipulates it with a knife. His sticky sculptures have been exhibited all over the world and have sold for as much as $70,000 each.

COLORFUL COLLECTION ■ Sculptor John McIntire of Memphis, Tennessee, donated 700 Hawaiian shirts—collected over the course of 50 years—to the Memphis College of Art.

LIST MANIA ■ Artist and author Hillary Carlip from Los Angeles, California, has been collecting abandoned shopping lists for many years, but in 2008 she took her hobby a step further by turning some of those lists into performance art. Realizing you can tell a lot about someone based on what they need at the grocery store— the way they write their list, their handwriting, and even the kind of paper they use—she concocted elaborate stories about the people who had written them, and then reinvented herself as those imaginary characters, dressing up and going to the store with their notes.

LEGO® OBAMA ■ Watched by more than 1,000 mini LEGO® people, a 4-in-high (10-cm) LEGO® model of Barack Obama was inaugurated in a replica presidential ceremony at LEGOLAND®, California, in January 2009. The detailed display also featured a LEGO® model White House, motorcade, and even people lining up outside the portable toilets.

FAVRE TRIBUTE ■ In 2008, Carlene and Duane Schultz of Eleva, Wisconsin, created a corn maze bearing the image of former Green Bay Packers quarterback Brett Favre to mark the announcement of his retirement. The maze reads "Thanks" and shows Favre's upper body holding a football, with his No. 4 jersey.

HAIR SCREEN ■ For an exhibition at Hanover, New Hampshire, New York City-based Chinese artist Wenda Gu created an 80 x 13 ft (24 x 4 m) screen made from human hair. It contained 430 lb (195 kg) of hair, collected over a period of several months from no less than 42,350 haircuts.

RUNNING EXHIBIT ■ A British artist who won the prestigious Turner Prize with lights that switched on and off and whose previous installations include a piece of putty stuck to a wall, unveiled his latest work in 2008—runners sprinting through a gallery. Martin Creed's creation consisted of 50 athletes taking turns to dash 282 ft (86 m) along London's Tate Britain gallery every 30 seconds for four months. He came up with the concept to illustrate that it is not necessary to look at paintings in a gallery for a long time.

CRAYON CANINE

Yellowdog *was made by Herb Williams from Tennessee who uses up to 250,000 coloring crayons to make each of his sculptures. His studio is filled from floor to ceiling with single-color boxes of 3,000 crayons delivered direct from the manufacturer.*

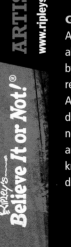

Flammable Faces

Careful how you handle these innovative sculptures by Scottish artist David Mach. His portraits of iconic figures are constructed from thousands of colored matchstick tips packed closely together to create 3-D heads. David created this sculpture of Elvis, 2 ft (60 cm) in height, using 50,000 matchsticks imported from Japan. Each match was glued on to a glass fiber-mold in a process that took more than 500 hours to complete. His other matchstick creations include Marilyn Monroe and a matchstick version of Michangelo's *David*. As a fitting end to his art, David sometimes takes a match to his sculptures and lets them disappear in flames.

GARAGE BOOTY ■ In January 2007, the American Folk Art Museum, in Manhattan, was about to stage an exhibition of rare drawings by Mexican artist Martín Ramírez when it received an e-mail on behalf of a woman from Auburn, California, saying she had some of his drawings—that had been lying in her garage for nearly two decades. In fact, she had 140 Ramírez artworks—and the total body of his previous known works only numbered 300. Some of his drawings have sold for more than $100,000.

MINI MONA ■ A British artist has painted a version of the *Mona Lisa* that is less than one-quarter the size of a postage stamp. Andrew Nicholls from Farnborough, Hampshire, painstakingly re-created Leonardo da Vinci's masterpiece in 1:70 scale to produce a replica just 7/16 in x ¼ in (11 x 7 mm). Peering through a magnifying glass, he used a 0000 gauge brush, which consisted of just a few strands of brush tapered to a fine point, to layer his acrylic paint on a piece of card.

CAN CREATIONS ■ A firm from Staffordshire, England, sells models of planes, trucks, and helicopters—all made from drinks cans. They will even personalize the gift using only cans from the recipient's favorite drink.

MATCHSTICK McLAREN ■ Michael Arndt from Hanover, Germany, spent six and a half years building a full-size model of a Formula One McLaren Mercedes racing car out of 956,000 matches. The car cost him $9,000 to build—that includes the 1,686 tubes of glue he used—and is ten layers thick in places so that it is strong enough to sit in.

BACK TO THEIR ROOTS ■ In March 2008, a train station in the Beatles' home city of Liverpool, England, unveiled life-sized sculptures of the Fab Four—carved out of a hedge. It took expert gardeners 18 months to grow the topiary John, Paul, George, and Ringo—plus their guitars and drum kit—and to shape the plants around handmade metal frames.

TOWERING CREATION ■ A matchstick model of London's famous Tower Bridge took Michael Williams of Shoebury, Essex, ten years to build—that's two years longer than the real bridge! He used more than 1.6 million wooden matchsticks—each painstakingly carved by hand—on his 6-ft-long (1.8-m) model, which has 156 working lights.

DIAMOND SKULL ■ In 2007, British artist Damien Hirst covered an 18th-century human skull with 8,601 diamonds—almost three times the number on the coronation crown of Queen Elizabeth II. The centerpiece of the $100 million artwork, titled *For the Love of God,* was a 52-carat stone set into the forehead, and even the eye sockets were filled with hundreds of jewels. The teeth were taken from the original skull before being polished and reset in the cast.

MATCH CLOCK ■ In 2008, David Harding of London, England, built a half-size grandmother clock from 12,000 matches.

SECURITY FILM ■ Using footage she obtained of herself that had been filmed by closed-circuit TV security systems in Britain, Austrian film-maker Manu Luksch created a movie called *Faceless.* In the movie, all the other faces are blocked out so that she is the only person with a recognizable human face.

HANGING RHINO ■ Made by Italian artist Stefano Bombardieri, a full-size sculpture of a rhinoceros hangs several feet above the ground in a street in Potsdam, Germany.

LITERARY VISION ■ Chinese author Chen Hong has written five novels—containing a total of 190,000 characters—despite having to dictate every word by blinking his eye. He was stricken with an incurable degenerative muscle disease in 1999, but manages to communicate with the help of a transparent board displaying phonetic symbols.

PAPER SHIP ■ Jared Shipman of Roseville, California, built a 320,000-piece model of the USS *Nimitz,* measuring 9 ft 1¾ in (2.78 m) in length, out of only paper.

LEAP DAY ■ Performance artist Brian Feldman from Orlando, Florida, marked Leap Day (29 February) 2008 by leaping off a platform 12 ft (3.6 m) high every 3 minutes 56 seconds over a 24-hour period. He managed to complete 366 leaps in all, to match the number of days in the "leap" year.

GUM SCULPTOR ■ Jamie Marraccini of Sterling, Virginia, makes ingenious works of art from chewing gum. Each sculpture contains hundreds—sometimes even thousands—of pieces of chewed gum molded into place. A collection of miniature human heads—titled *Fiesta de Huevos*—used 804 pieces of gum, while Marraccini used 4,212 pieces to make a 2 x 3 ft (60 x 90 cm) gum portrait of himself and his wife, which he took five years to complete. Although he can chew 50 pieces a day, Marraccini needs help with supplies and so hands out packs of gum to workmates and friends, along with laminated sheets of paper on which the willing helpers can return the chewed gum. He then groups the gum into color categories before using it in a sculpture.

DIAL-A-DRESS ■ In 2008, Jolis Paons, an innovative student at Indiana University's Herron School of Art and Design, made a lightweight dress constructed entirely out of pages from phonebooks.

PLASTIC FANTASTIC ■ Artist Brian Jungen from Vancouver, British Columbia, Canada, created life-sized statues of whale skeletons made entirely from white plastic deck chairs. He specializes in turning everyday objects into works of art and has also created elaborate ceremonial native masks from running shoes.

FASHION BUG ■ When swarms of cicadas invaded the town of Sandwich, Massachusetts, in the summer of 2008, two enterprising teenagers saw a business opportunity and turned the dead insects into jewelry. Katheryn Moloney and Brady Cullinan charged $10 for a pair of earrings or a necklace made out of the lacquered carcasses of the bugs.

PAINTED SNAILS ■ In 2008, an artist calling himself Slinkachu, from London, England, used nontoxic paints to decorate live snails' shells in pretty colors and patterns as part of a series of designs dubbed "Inner City Snail—a slow-moving street art project."

mini art

Vladimir Aniskin takes miniature art to a whole new level of tiny. Rejecting canvas and normal paintbrushes, the Russian artist uses human hairs, poppy seeds, and grape seeds and, unbelievably, casts shoes for the feet of real fleas that he picked off his cat. His pieces have to be seen—or not seen—to be believed!

Vladimir works as a scientific researcher by day, and does all of his micro-miniature artwork with the help of a microscope. It is a painstaking discipline and he rises early each morning before going to work to make his creations, working between heartbeats to keep an incredibly steady hand. He has placed a caravan of seven camels walking along the eye of a needle, each one only 0.0039 in (0.1 mm) high, and written out a classic Russian story, comprising 2,027 letters over 22 lines, quite clearly on a grain of rice.

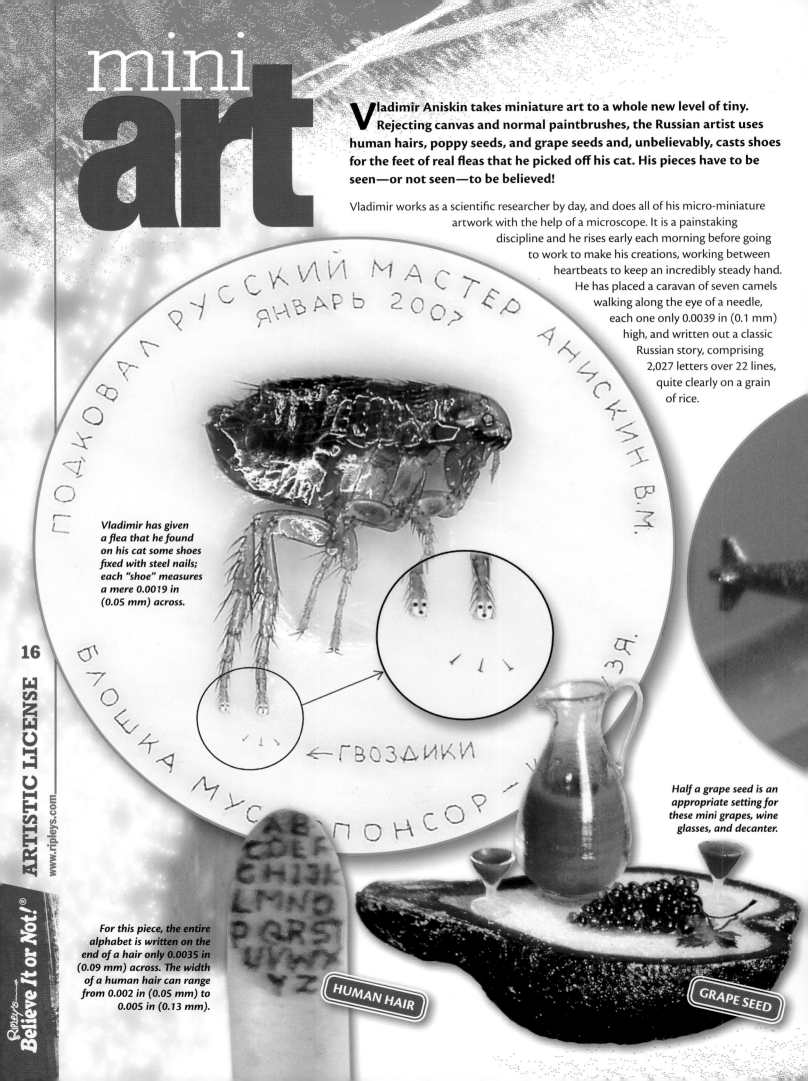

ПОДКОВАЛ РУССКИЙ МАСТЕР АНИСКИН В.М.
ЯНВАРЬ 2007

БЛОШКА МУСА ... ПОНСОР ...

← ГВОЗДИКИ

Vladimir has given a flea that he found on his cat some shoes fixed with steel nails; each "shoe" measures a mere 0.0019 in (0.05 mm) across.

Half a grape seed is an appropriate setting for these mini grapes, wine glasses, and decanter.

For this piece, the entire alphabet is written on the end of a hair only 0.0035 in (0.09 mm) across. The width of a human hair can range from 0.002 in (0.05 mm) to 0.005 in (0.13 mm).

HUMAN HAIR

GRAPE SEED

POPPY SEED

For this seasonal piece, Vladimir placed a snowman measuring 0.0019 in (0.055-mm) high on half a poppy seed, under a banner supported by specks of dust.

С НОВЫМ ГОДОМ!

2006

HUMAN HAIR

A tiny submarine 0.015 in (0.39 mm) long on the end of a strand of horsehair and made of platinum.

A rosebud made of dust particles, only 0.002 in (0.065 mm) across and set inside a human hair like a glass vase.

HORSEHAIR

MATCH

The scale of Vladimir's work can be seen when comparing a matchstick head to a ⅛-in-long (3.5-mm) chess table, complete with gold and silver chess pieces as small as 0.006 in (0.15 mm).

Ripley's ask

Why did you start making miniature art?

In 1998, I accidentally came across a book about Soviet masters of microminiature art. I was impressed by the works that were described. Within myself, the desire arose to make something similar. The book did not describe the technology of making microminiatures; one thing was clear—I needed a microscope. Soon I managed to get a child's one-eyed microscope. It was extremely difficult to work with: it turned the representation from right to left and upside down. Finally, I managed to obtain a good binocular microscope, and I work with it to this day.

What problems do you have in your work?

The main difficulty in microminiature is one's heartbeat. If you use a needle with your fingertips, calm yourself and breathe smoothly, the tip of the needle begins to flutter to the beat of your heart. It is impossible to get rid of such fluctuation. You can only adapt to it—that is, to do particularly delicate work between the heartbeats. Another difficulty in microminiature-making is static electricity. It happens sometimes that the material sticks to the tool, and it is impossible to separate it without damaging it.

What materials and tools do you use?

Perhaps all materials are suitable for microminiature art. Each of them has its own properties, which can be successfully used in each particular case. Longevity is the main issue for the use of any material. If a material can undergo oxidation, it cannot be used. For instance, copper should not be used. Unfortunately. even specialists are unable to predict the behavior of material at micro levels; we all have to learn by experience. Some materials are particularly sensitive to moisture—for example, hair. The works Camels in a Hair and Rose in a Hair have been repaired several times.

How small do you think you can make art in the future?

If you consider the principle of microminiature, "small, even smaller, the smallest in the world," we can say the following: the objects to which you can apply this slogan should be easily recognizable by everybody. This can be, for example, chess, books, or musical instruments. A micro violin must contain all the standard parts of a regular violin. When one reaches smaller and smaller dimensions, it is important to distinguish between art and modern methods of nanotechnology. Art is what is made solely by the human hand. In making microminiatures, I can identify several objectives worthy of hard work. This is the smallest alphabet, the smallest book, chess, musical instruments, or other smallest objects made by the hand of man.

Do you have any ambitions for your miniature art?

I am planning to continue a series of micro-military orders that reflect the military honor of the Russian nation, as well as a series of Russian cartoon characters.

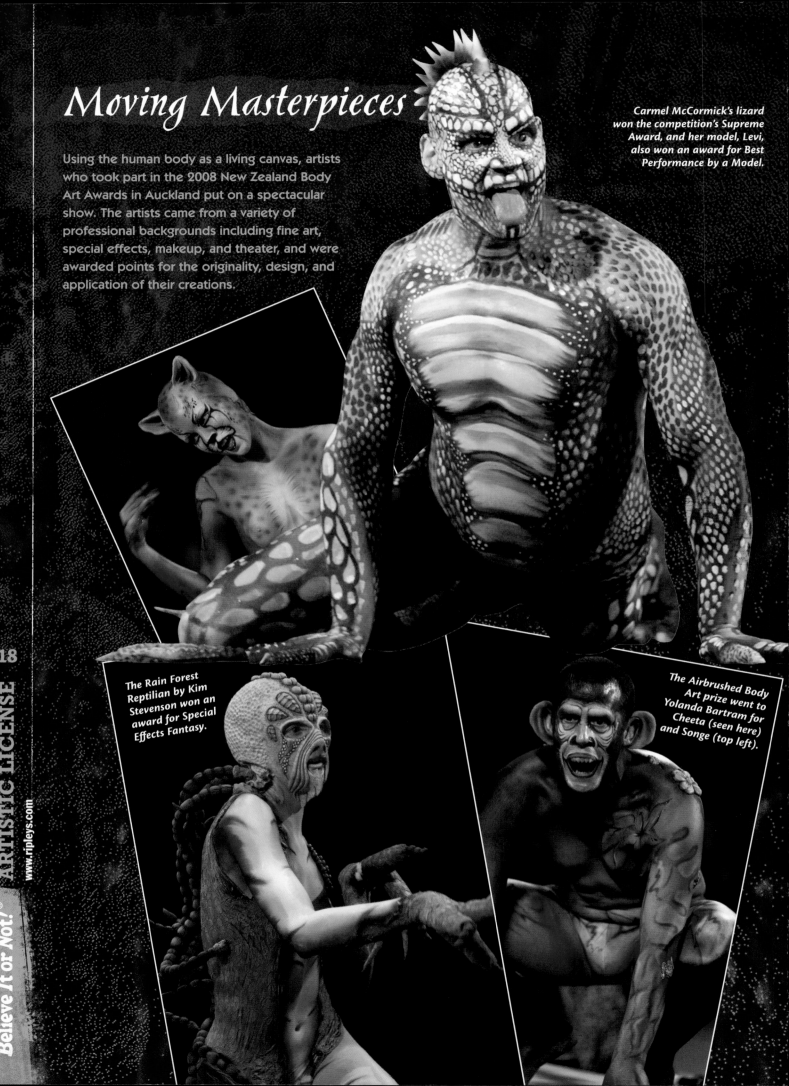

Moving Masterpieces

Using the human body as a living canvas, artists who took part in the 2008 New Zealand Body Art Awards in Auckland put on a spectacular show. The artists came from a variety of professional backgrounds including fine art, special effects, makeup, and theater, and were awarded points for the originality, design, and application of their creations.

Carmel McCormick's lizard won the competition's Supreme Award, and her model, Levi, also won an award for Best Performance by a Model.

The Rain Forest Reptilian by Kim Stevenson won an award for Special Effects Fantasy.

The Airbrushed Body Art prize went to Yolanda Bartram for Cheeta (seen here) and Songe (top left).

ARTISTIC LICENSE

www.ripleys.com

Ripley's
Believe It or Not!®

LONG LINE ■ At Ireland's Rockland County Feis and Field Games in July 2008, 312 dancers stretched out to form a continuous dancing line that was more than 700 ft (213 m) long.

STOP-START ART Performance artist Matthew Keeney walked from the Capitol steps in Washington, D.C., to the Lincoln Memorial and back in February 2008, stopping each time he heard a car horn and then starting again when he heard another. The 3.8-mi (6-km) walk took him just under 3 hours.

SHARK PHOBIA ■ Hollywood actress Christina Ricci suffers from pool-selachophobia—she's scared that a shark might swim through a hatch in the side of a swimming pool.

ARTISTIC TYPE ■ Israeli artist and typographer Oded Ezer creates startling works of art from typefaces, especially Hebrew fonts. His short film, *The Finger*, presents an imaginary landscape composed of Hebrew letters.

PLAY-A-DAY ■ The New York City Off-Broadway Show, *365 Days/365 Plays*, is a compilation of the 365 plays that American playwright Suzan-Lori Parks wrote in 365 days.

PRIVATE CONCERT ■ A violinist who left a 285-year-old Stradivarius on the back seat of a New York City cab in April 2008 played a special concert to thank the driver who returned it to him. Philippe Quint accidentally left the $4-million violin in the airport taxi after a performance in Dallas, but following an appeal, driver Mohamed Khalil got in touch the next day to return it. The grateful violinist gave the driver a $100 tip and free tickets to his next New York concert and a 30-minute private performance in the taxi waiting area at Newark Liberty International Airport.

BRAD'S BAN ■ American actor Brad Pitt is banned from ever entering China because of his role in the movie *Seven Years in Tibet*.

ICE PIANO ■ As part of the 20th International Snow-Sculpture Art Expo in Harbin, China, during the winter of 2007–08, a company designed and built an ice piano that could be played by visitors. The life-size ice sculpture could also automatically play more than 30 classic piano pieces before, come the warmer spring, it melted away.

CHANGE OF CLOTHES ■ David Whitthoft of Ridgefield, Connecticut, wore a football jersey every day for 1,581 days straight—more than four years—before finally taking it off on his 12th birthday, April 23, 2008.

QUICK PICKER ■ Despite suffering from a rare muscular disorder, Todd Taylor of Palm Bay, Florida, can play the banjo at 210 beats per minute. A typical fast bluegrass song is 130 bpm. He demonstrated his skill by playing "Duelling Banjos"—a piece normally performed by two people—at such a pace that he had to superglue the picks to his fingers to stop them flying off. He is such a fast player that he has to change the strings of his banjo three times a day.

PERCUSSION POWER ■ Akron, Ohio, musician Link Logen played the drums for 86 hours 16 minutes straight in June/July 2008—that's more than three-and-a-half days. He survived the lack of sleep largely on coffee but at one point started crying because of the extreme mental and physical fatigue. "As I was playing," he said, "I literally went into a catatonic state."

BEAUTIFUL DAY ■ A painting that hung in U2's recording studio in Dublin was sold at auction for $10 million in 2008—19 years after it was spotted by the Irish rock band's bass player, Adam Clayton, in a New York gallery. The painting was "Pecho/Oreja" by American graffiti artist Jean-Michel Basquiat.

BEAR SUIT ■ A British artist produced a two-hour film that showed him spending ten nights in a Berlin museum while dressed in a bear suit. Mark Wallinger said that wearing the bear suit in the film, entitled *Sleeper*, enabled him to "look through the eyes of something that was of another culture."

PRIZED POEMS ■ A signed collection of poetry by William McGonagall (1825–1902), known as "The World's Worst Poet," sold at an auction in Edinburgh, Scotland, in May 2008, for £6,600 (more than $10,000),—more than the selling price for a first-edition signed set of Harry Potter books.

BARGAIN BURIAL ■ To save costs, the body of William Shakespeare's friend and fellow dramatist Ben Jonson was buried standing up in Westminster Abbey in 1637.

[GUM WRAPPERS] Vanessa Randall of Wayne, Maine, made her 2008 high-school prom dress from 3,000 gum wrappers. She started collecting the wrappers three years earlier, helped by friends and family.

BIRTHDAY PRESENT ■ Robert Louis Stevenson, author of *Treasure Island*, willed his birthday, November 13, to a friend because she was born on Christmas Day and never had a birthday celebration.

CANOE TOPIARY ■ Glenn Tabor of Leeds, England, has created something different in his front garden—a topiary sculpture of a huge Native American man paddling a 16-ft (5-m) canoe. "I was bored with having a normal hedge," he says, "and decided we should have something a bit eccentric." He used manual shears and an electric hedge-trimmer to make his creation.

LIBRARY LABOR ■ Polish historian Jan Alvertrandy (1731–1808), forbidden to copy historical documents from libraries in Upsala and Stockholm, Sweden, memorized the entire contents of 100 volumes. He read them day by day in the library and then wrote down every word he had learned at night.

HEAVY READING ■ The book *Greatest of All Time*, a tribute to boxer Muhammad Ali, is itself a heavyweight. It weighs in at an astonishing 75 lb (34 kg). Furthermore, it contains 3,000 pictures and nearly 600,000 words.

WHEAT MODELS ■ Scale models of British landmarks were unveiled in 2007—made from wheat. London's Big Ben clock tower, the Blackpool Tower, and Edinburgh Castle were among the eight structures re-created in wheat for an exhibition aptly entitled "Land of Wheat and Glory."

MUSICAL METHANE ■ Practicing yoga with his sister, Paul Oldfield from Macclesfield, Cheshire, England, developed a talent of his own that would eventually lead to him blowing away audiences as the world's only full-time performing flatulist. Oldfield, who calls himself Mr. Methane, found that he could control his gas emissions to mimic the sounds of such diverse tunes as Johann Strauss's "The Blue Danube" waltz and Kylie Minogue's pop hit "I Should Be So Lucky."

FALL GUY ■ Four scaffolding waterfalls installed as an art project on New York City's East River in 2008 churned 2.1 million gal (8 million l) of water per hour. Designed by Dutch artist Olafur Eliasson, the tallest artificial waterfall was 120 ft (37 m) in height and the widest was 30 ft (9 m) wide. Eliasson is no stranger to mimicking nature. He had previously re-created the Sun in London's Tate Modern gallery with the help of 2,000 yellow lamps and numerous mirrors.

COMEDY ROUTINE ■ More than 80 comedians performed a nonstop comedy routine for 50 hours at New York City's Comic Strip in June 2008.

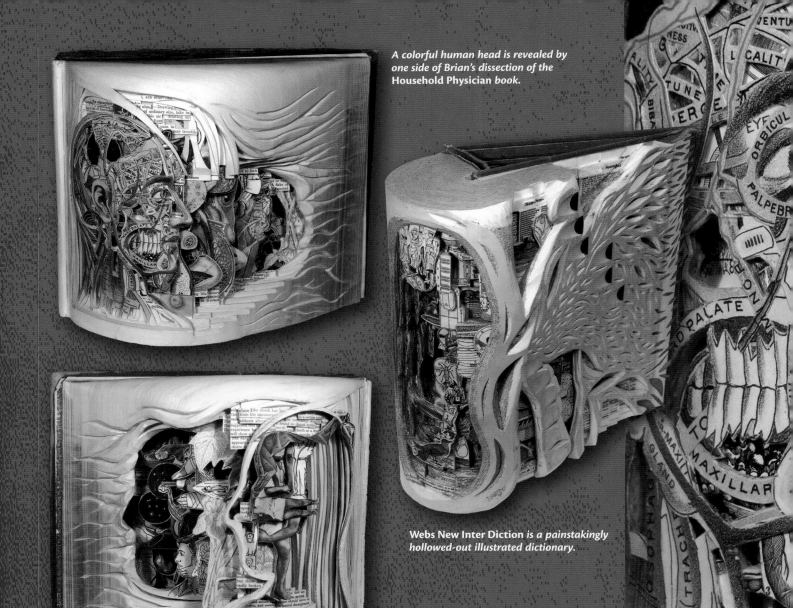

A *colorful human head is revealed by one side of Brian's dissection of the* **Household Physician** *book.*

Webs New Inter Diction *is a painstakingly hollowed-out illustrated dictionary.*

The other side of **Household Physician** *displays equally intricate work.*

ARTISTIC LICENSE

www.ripleys.com

MURDER MYSTERY ■ The publication of his debut novel *Amok* led to Polish author Krystian Bala being jailed for 25 years in 2007. A court decided that his murder-mystery novel was too close to the truth, after it was discovered that the supposedly fictional story bore striking similarities to a real-life incident in which Bala had allegedly tortured and killed a businessman seven years previously.

HIDDEN TALENT ■ Dutch artist Desiree Palmen creates amazing camouflage art by wearing suits that are hand-painted so that they exactly match her chosen background. First, Desiree photographs a scene and then she uses acrylic paints to meticulously transfer its detail on to a cotton suit. The artist then poses in the suit against the chosen backdrop—and immediately becomes virtually invisible.

TRAVEL FATIGUE ■ In 2008, technicians at a museum in Madrid identified 129 changes to Pablo Picasso's famous anti-war painting *Guernica*, caused by wear and tear from its many journeys around the world. Painted in 1937, the 11 x 25 ft (3.4 x 7.6 m) canvas was exhibited in dozens of cities on both sides of the Atlantic over the following 20 years.

SLOW READ ■ Ante Matec of Zagreb, Croatia, borrowed a book in 1967 and never got around to reading it. He returned it in 2007!

YOUNG WRITER ■ By the age of eight, English poet and writer Thomas Babington Macaulay (1800–1859) had penned a compendium of world history as well as "The Battle of Cheviot," a romantic narrative poem in the style of Sir Walter Scott.

BIDDING WAR ■ A painting sold for 1,700 times its maximum reserve price in 2007, because the winning bidder decided it was a self-portrait by the 17th-century Dutch artist Rembrandt. The painting—*The Young Rembrandt as Democrates the Laughing Philosopher*—was valued at just $3,400 by experts who considered that it was not by Rembrandt himself. So inconsequential was it that it had hung in a house in Gloucestershire, England, for several years. Yet at a London auction it fetched a staggering $5.8 million.

CAN CAN CHAIR ■ British interior designer Laurence Llewelyn-Bowen has created a stylish modern armchair entirely from recycled drinks cans. He designed the "Can Can Chair" using nothing but cans that he and his family collected from around the house.

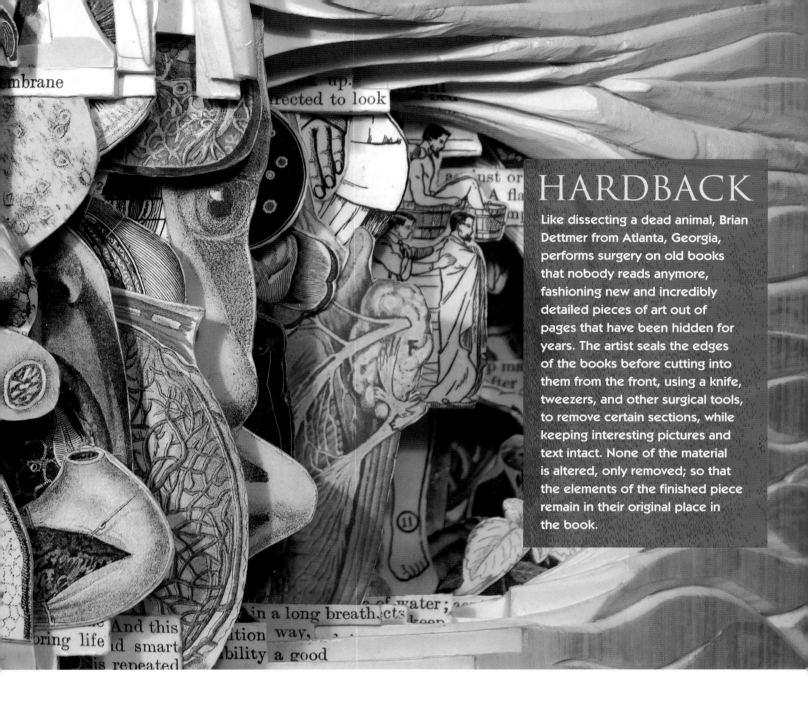

HARDBACK

Like dissecting a dead animal, Brian Dettmer from Atlanta, Georgia, performs surgery on old books that nobody reads anymore, fashioning new and incredibly detailed pieces of art out of pages that have been hidden for years. The artist seals the edges of the books before cutting into them from the front, using a knife, tweezers, and other surgical tools, to remove certain sections, while keeping interesting pictures and text intact. None of the material is altered, only removed; so that the elements of the finished piece remain in their original place in the book.

BOOK SENTENCE ■ Keely Givhan of Beloit, Wisconsin, spent six days in jail in 2008—for having overdue library books.

SOLD SISTER ■ In 2004, British singer James Blunt sold his sister on eBay! He asked for a knight in shining armor to bid for a damsel in distress when his sister couldn't find transport to attend a funeral in Ireland. The winning bidder offered her the use of his private helicopter, and three years later the couple actually married!

HEAD LICE ■ Seven young artists from Berlin, Germany, with lice in their hair, lived in an Israeli museum for three weeks in 2008. The artists, who slept, ate, and bathed in the gallery and who wore plastic shower caps to prevent the lice from spreading, said their exhibition fitted in with a theme of hosts and guests.

RARE VOLUME ■ The only privately owned copy of the 711-year-old Magna Carta (an English legal charter) was sold to an investment company in 2007—for more than $21 million.

DRUM ROLL ■ Eric Sader Jr. of Salina, Kansas, played a continuous drum roll for 1 hour 22 minutes 5 seconds at McPherson College in May 2008.

RUBBER ART ■ Artist Chakaia Booker from New York City creates sculptures from old tires. She salvages them from streets, gas stations, auto body shops, and recycling centers.

HEAVY DUTY ■ No wonder fame sometimes hung heavy on his shoulders—some of Elvis Presley's bejewelled jumpsuits weighed more than 30 lb (12 kg)!

AUTO PARTS ■ An auto parts shop in Moscow, Russia, decorated its forecourt with sculptures of people made solely from the spare parts of used cars.

DEATH CHANNEL ■ A television channel devoted almost exclusively to death has been launched in Germany. Eos TV, run by producer Wolf Tilmann Schneider in conjunction with Germany's funeral association, is screened 24 hours a day, 7 days a week, on cable and the Internet, and its program lineup includes televised obituaries plus numerous documentaries about graveyards.

HIDDEN TREASURE ■ Elizabeth Gibson of New York City found a painting in a garbage pile that was actually a stolen work by Mexican artist Rufino Tamayo and worth over $1 million.

LIFE IN BLACK AND WHITE

Maverick artist Scott Blake creates well-known portraits made up from hundreds of humble bar-code bars.

He started to think about using bar codes in art around the time of the Y2K scare. While manipulating images on a computer, he discovered that some of the patterns resembled bar codes, and he decided to make portraits of famous faces using the everyday black-and-white lines that we usually ignore. Scott's first piece of bar-code art was of Jesus—he manipulated 940 barcodes over 48 sheets of paper and stuck them together to complete the face. A portrait of Elvis consists of hundreds of bar codes from real-life Elvis Presley products.

Scott has also created interactive pieces where scanning the bar codes on a portrait of an icon such as Bruce Lee or Elvis flashes up images of them on a screen. When scanned, every bar code on the picture of Bruce Lee will play a fight scene from one of his movies. Scott also works with tattoos, flipbooks, and online art using bar codes. These include an automatic counter that will run through every possible bar-code number combination— over 100,000,000,000—for more than 300 years.

A bar-code portrait of martial-arts legend and movie star Bruce Lee has formed part of an interactive piece by Scott.

7 82086

The further you hold the page away from your eyes, the clearer the King becomes.

BIZARRE BAR CODES

> The first patent for a bar code was issued in 1952. The very first bar codes were orange and blue stripes, used to keep track of freight-train cars as they traveled around the United States.

> International insect experts are interested in placing miniature bar codes on bees to help track more than 20,000 different species of bee.

> The first two numbers of a bar code always identify the country of origin. Each number of the bar code is represented by two black and two white bars of varying widths, which the scanner reads.

> The U.S. Army has used bar codes up to 2 ft (60 cm) in length to label large boats in docks.

Scott uses the bar codes at varying sizes to create the desired effect.

Scott's interpretation of Jesus, made from bar codes.

Scott standing in front of his portrait of Jesus.

Jason's **Beach Trumpet** *on a beach in Portland, Oregon.*

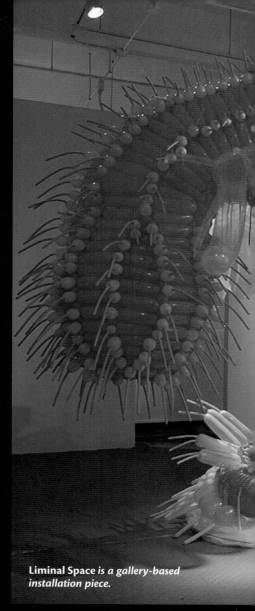

Liminal Space *is a gallery-based installation piece.*

24
ARTISTIC LICENSE
www.ripleys.com
e It or Not!®

Beautiful Balloons

New York City artist Jason Hackenwerth creates surreal, mystical creatures—such as giant plants and alien monsters—solely from balloons. He spends up to $12,000 a year on balloons for his creations, which can be made from around 3,000 individual balloons and take 25 hours of work. Luckily, less than 10 percent of the balloons pop. Jason's sculptures are inspired by living creatures and human anatomy, and can last for months in the right conditions.

PEN PORTRAITS ■ Kenyan artist Troy Howe re-creates classic paintings with a ballpoint pen. Taking up to 16 hours on each work, he has drawn pen versions of Leonardo da Vinci's *Mona Lisa*, Johannes Vermeer's *Girl with a Pearl Earring,* and a portrait of the U.K.'s Queen Elizabeth II.

EXPENSIVE PITCHER ■ A priceless 1,000-year-old Egyptian carved rock-crystal pitcher sold for around $6 million in England in October 2008—nine months after nearly being sold for just $200. A Somerset auction house had wrongly identified it as a 19th-century French claret jug, but luckily for the owner the

DESK CARVINGS ■ Chris Reeves from Hertfordshire, England, carved a complete nativity scene—including beautiful 3-ft-high (90-cm) wooden figurines of Mary, Joseph, and the Angel Gabriel—from a pile of old schoolroom desks.

EDIBLE NATIVITY ■ A farm shop in Crawley, Sussex, England, staged a nativity scene at Christmas 2008 with all the characters made from fruit and vegetables. The Three Wise Men were made of squash, onions, and apples, Mary and Joseph were made from butternut squash with lemon crowns, sheep were created from cauliflower florets, and baby Jesus was

DUMPSTER PARK ■ Oliver Bishop-Young from London, England, creates urban artworks in dumpsters. He has turned the yellow containers into a skateboard park, a swimming pool, a living room, and even a miniature park complete with a park bench.

FOOD COVERS ■ A Japanese website has featured dozens of famous CD album covers made using traditional lunchbox food such as seaweed, egg, potatoes, and ham—all on a standard rice base. Album-cover designs by the Obacchi Jacket Lunch Box site include *Voodoo Lounge* by the Rolling Stones and *In Utero* by Nirvana.

TOPIARY PUDDING ■ Roger and Valerie Holley from Somerset, England, spent five years creating a 20-ft-high (6-m) topiary Christmas pudding in their front garden. They merged and pruned two conifer trees into a round shape before adding plywood leaves, and berries made

www.ripleybooks.com
@ go to >>>>

Paper Faces

Dutch artist Bert Simons has cloned himself in paper. The Rotterdam sculptor makes realistic, lifesize, 3-D paper models of human heads with the aid of computer technology. He first creates a computer model of his subject and then flattens it into its component parts. Once a template is created, he prints it out on a sheet of paper ready to be cut out and reassembled (see below). By this method he has also created models of friends and even a turtle.

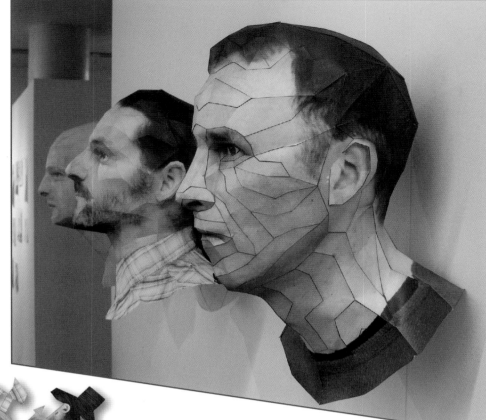

Cookie City

A model city 16 ft (5 m) long, 16 ft (5 m) wide, and 8 ft (2.5 m) high was unveiled in Shenyang, China, at the end of 2007. The edible edifice was made with 25,000 cookies, weighed over 2,200 lb (1,000 kg) and featured many famous landmarks from the city, including the Imperial Palace and the TV tower.

GAS STATEMENT ■ Sick of paying high gas prices and irritated by the abandoned gas station that was causing an eyesore on her drive, artist Jennifer Marsh from DeWitt, New York, decided to cover it with a vast handmade blanket. Helped by artists from 15 countries and by more than 2,500 grade-school students in 29 states, Marsh covered the 5,000 sq ft (465 sq m) of the station. including the pumps, light stands, and signs, with more than 3,000 colorful panels that were crocheted, knitted, or stitched together to form a single blanket. The panels were made from such diverse materials as leather, silk, and plastic shopping bags.

CLIP ART ■ American artist Joshua Mantyla creates sculptures from paper clips. He started off by making simple flowers, but has since progressed to such intricate artworks as a small motorcycle—complete with rotating wheels—and an oversized 3-ft (90-cm) mouse, the latter taking him some 3,000 hours to complete.

STYROFOAM PRESIDENT ■ In 2007, Fran Volz of Arlington Heights, Illinois, unveiled a Styrofoam sculpture of Abraham Lincoln. It took eight months to create the 250-lb (113-kg), 10-ft (3-m) sculpture, which was carved with the aid of an electric chainsaw.

ARTISTIC LICENSE

With stunts that definitely come under the heading "Don't do this at home," Chinese photographer and performance artist Li Wei appears to defy gravity.

One minute he is floating horizontally from a window on the 29th floor of a Beijing skyscraper, the next he is buried at an angle of almost 45 degrees with his head through the windshield of a car or he is submerged vertically, headfirst in a lake.

Li Wei's spectacular self-portraits, which sell for up to $8,000, do not use computer software. Instead, the 38-year-old farmer's son from Beijing often risks life and limb, using invisible steel wire supports to hang in midair vast distances above the ground.

Other photos are created with the help of a 3-ft-sq (0.3-sq-m) mirror with a hole in the center large enough to accommodate his head and neck. He then places his head through the hole and projects his image onto various historical and urban settings.

Li Wei has taken his hair-raising performances all over the world—to the U.S.A., Italy, Spain, Australia and Korea—including a series of startling photographs showing him crashing into walls and sidewalks.

It may seem that Li Wei has already achieved the ultimate in death-defying art, but his aim is to take it to a higher level by hovering from even taller buildings.

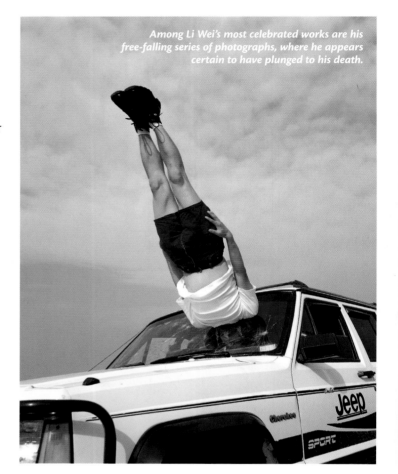

Among Li Wei's most celebrated works are his free-falling series of photographs, where he appears certain to have plunged to his death.

Li Wei defies gravity by standing on his head in Hong Kong's Victoria Harbor.

Ripley's ask

Why did you start performance art?

I studied oil painting first. In 1996, I started to do performance art. In the beginning, I used photos and video works only to record my performance art. Later, I turned to photography.

How do you describe your art?

My photos always immortalize me at the very limits of the absurd and are stupendous for their originality that, at times, borders on madness. My form of artistic experimentation is a metaphor for a restless existential state that puts stress on our physical condition by putting it to the test and going beyond the limits of human resistance.

How do you suspend yourself in the air?

I use iron wire on my back to hang myself up.

Is any of your work dangerous?

Yes, it's dangerous. That's why I'm fascinated with it.

What kind of reactions do the photos get? Are people scared by them?

People love my work. They react in different ways. Some think it humorous and others think it unique.

What are your future plans?

I'll try 3-D animation and also statues. I've made some statues full of broken mirrors. I'll do more and more in the future. Also, I won't stop performance art.

Wires strapped to Li Wei's back enable him to hover from skyscrapers.

In addition to wire supports, Li Wei uses his acrobatic skills to achieve striking poses.

MAIZE MAZE ■ In 2008, a British farmer created a maze in the shape of the Statue of Liberty that was nearly 12 times bigger than the statue itself. Using more than a million corn stalks, Tom Pearcy cut a 437-yd-long (400-m) outline of the famous statue in a field near the city of York. His past patterns have included a Viking ship and London's Big Ben clock.

RADIO TWEET ■ A temporary U.K. radio station with nothing but a 20-minute loop recording of birdsong picked up half a million listeners in early 2008.

CHALK TRAIN ■ In January 2009, more than 2,000 schoolchildren and teachers in Cluj, Romania, helped create a drawing on a deserted highway that stretched to around 4 mi (6.4 km) in length. They used 10,000 boxes of colored chalks to draw a 7,000-yd-long train.

POINTLESS TRIP ■ Before making his 1934 epic *Cleopatra*, Cecil B. DeMille sent a team of researchers on a $100,000 trip to Egypt to study the color of the Pyramids—even though the film was in black and white.

KARAOKE MARATHON ■ Anthony Lawson of Wilmington, North Carolina, sang karaoke songs for more than 39 hours straight in June 2008.

JUMBO PROJECT ■ Mark Coreth of Wiltshire, England, has built a full-size sculpture of an African bull elephant in his garden. He created the skeleton of the 13-ft-high (4-m) elephant out of chicken wire before filling it in with polystyrene and giving it a coat of plaster and a bronze finish. It weighs six tons and is so heavy that he needed scaffolding to support the elephant while he was working on it.

METALLIC CLOTHS ■ Ghanaian sculptor El Anatsui specializes in making huge cloths from various recycled objects such as bottle caps, labels, and washers. He once created an 18-ft (5.5-m) wide, 16-ft (5-m) high tapestry of aluminum liquor-bottle labels bound together with copper wire and followed that with another giant shimmering cloth, this time made by stitching together thousands of whiskey bottle caps.

MELTING COW ■ In Budapest, Hungary, there is a plastic sculpture of a blue cow that appears to be melting on the ground in the heat. The cow sculpture takes the form of a melting ice cream and even has a stick emerging from the animal's rear.

Knit Knot Tree
Offbeat artists Nancy Mellon and Corrine Bayraktaroglu made sure a tree in Yellow Springs, Ohio, was warm through the winter when they knitted a sweater to cover its branches. The unusual piece of clothing started as a single knitted section and grew day by day, with people adding pockets and vivid colors. It soon began to attract attention from people all around the world.

PHOTO OPPORTUNITY ■ Matt Frondorf of San Antonio, Texas, drove across the United States from New York to San Francisco—a distance of more than 3,300 mi (5,310 km)— taking a photograph every mile along the way.

PHONEY SHEEP ■ French artist Jean-Luc Cornec exhibits life-sized sculptures of sheep made from recycled telephones and curly phone cables. The twisted cables replicate the wool of the sheep while the old-style phone receiver placed on its rest is used to represent the sheep's head.

PEN FRIENDS ■ Juan Francisco Casas, a Spanish artist living in Rome, illustrates portraits that stand up to 10 ft (3 m) tall—using nothing but blue ballpoint pens. Casas, who started out as a traditional painter, often uses just four cheap ballpoints—costing less than a dollar in total—on one picture, but his works sell for around $7,500.

LIMESTONE LIONESS ■ *The Guennol Lioness*, a 5,000-year-old sculpture from Mesopotamia, sold for $57.2 million in an auction in December 2007 in New York City. The tiny limestone figure, which measures just 3¼ in (8.3 cm) tall, had been on loan to the Brooklyn Museum of Art since 1948.

BLINKING DICTATION ■ Despite being almost entirely paralyzed following a massive stroke, French author Jean-Dominique Bauby wrote his 1997 book *The Diving Bell and the Butterfly* by blinking his left eyelid! A friend slowly recited the alphabet over and over again, and Bauby blinked when the friend reached the required letter, meaning that the book was written one letter at a time. Three days after it was published, Bauby died from heart failure.

DECK-CHAIR DESIGNS ■ Artists and celebrities dreamed up colorful designs as part of an exhibition of 700 deck chairs in London's city parks over the summer of 2008. The oldest designer was 98-year-old Fleur Cowles, a London-based American who was once a friend of the Spanish artist Picasso.

DANNY BOY ■ The song "Danny Boy" was performed continuously for 50 hours at a Ferndale, Michigan, coffee shop in March 2008. There were nearly 1,000 renditions, including classical, folk, blues, rap, spoken word, and foreign language versions of the song, played on a variety of instruments including piano, trombone, violin, and kazoo.

MONSTER MURAL ■ In 2008, a group of 510 students from a university in Luoyang, Henan Province, China, created a mural of flowers that covered 5,490 sq ft (510 sq m). The color painting consisted of 170 three-ply boards and measured 62 x 80 ft (20.8 x 24.5 m).

CAT HAT ■ A grandmother has set up a thriving business by making hats from the feral cats that roam the remote Tasmanian island where she lives. Each week Robyn Eades takes delivery of frozen cat carcasses—shot by a local ranger to cull the population—and they are then defrosted and skinned before being tanned and stitched into winter hats, coat-hangers, and purses. Her designs are so popular that she has taken orders from as far away as Siberia. She says: "I feel like I am saving them from their fate. They are going to live forever in my creations."

LONG DRAW ■ For more than a year, Mexican artist Filemon Trevino devoted all his energies to creating a pencil drawing that was ¼ mi (0.5 km) long. He spent 6,000 hours and used 800 pencils to complete his representation of the heart and circulatory system, which incorporated doves and geometric shapes. He worked so hard he lost 35 lb (16 kg) in weight and was hospitalized seven times for dehydration, heart and kidney problems, and fainting spells.

QUAKE ALARM ■ In March 2007, musicians in the Japanese city of Omi played a concert that lasted for 182 hours—that's more than a week—despite a major earthquake rocking the venue during the piano piece. Performers ranging in age from six to 96 took turns in playing some 2,000 tunes, but the most impressive musician was the unflappable pianist. "She was amazing," said one of the organizers." The whole place was shaking quite badly, but she went right on playing. Even an earthquake couldn't stop us."

RHYMING COUPLETS ■ Dr. Mulki Radhakrishna Shetty of Bangalore, India, wrote 50,000 rhyming couplets in just 24 months.

SUICIDE SCARE ■ A Chinese artist sparked a suicide scare in 2008 by hanging naked mannequins from the outside of Shanghai skyscrapers. Liu Jin positioned four mannequins with wings on their backs for his work *Wounded Angels*, but passersby mistook them for real people who looked as if they were about to jump.

INTERNET CHAT ■ In 2008, artists Ben Rubin and Mark Hansen created a work of art to replicate 100,000 people chatting online. The visual and sonic installation at London's Science Museum involved 231 small electronic screens.

HUMAN COMPUTER ■ Thomas Watts (1811–69), librarian of the British Museum in London, memorized the full title and exact location of every one of the volumes the museum acquired between 1851 and 1860—a total of 680,000 books.

THE BIG ONE! ■ Angler Mike Wallis of Warner, Oklahoma, must have been hoping to hook the big one! He built a steel fishing rod 83 ft (25 m) long with a fully functioning reel.

MASTER SAMPLER ■ British D.J. Osymyso (a.k.a. Mark Nicholson) sampled 50 different songs in one track in 2008. He had previously created "Intro-Inspection," which put intros to 101 well-known songs into a 12-minute track.

Henk's egg creations were so large that children could sit high up on the yolks.

Sunny Side Up

Fried eggs measuring 100 ft (30 m) wide were the order of the day when Dutch artist Henk Hofstra left them on city squares in Leeuwarden, Holland, for six months in 2008 as part of a city project. The artist dubbed his creations the *Art Eggcident*, and is no stranger to unusual artistic stunts, having once painted an entire street blue.

FISHY IDEA ■ Girls in Chengdu, China, latched on to a new fashion craze in 2008—wearing live fish around their necks as jewelry. They queued in their hundreds to buy sealed plastic pendants housing the fish, which can live there for three months, because the pendants contain water, fish food, and two solid oxygen balls. At the end of the three months, the fish can be released.

MOWNA LISA ■ Tania Ledger from London, England, hired a 3-D art expert to re-create the "Mona Lisa" in grass in her front garden. Chris Naylor took two days to reproduce Leonardo da Vinci's masterpiece, using a small lawn mower and garden tools.

SUSHI MOSAIC ■ Twenty students in Mumbai, India, made a sushi mosaic measuring 163 sq ft (15.16 sq m) using 5,814 pieces of sushi in March 2008.

SALVEST SALVAGE ■ Jonesboro, Arkansas, artist John Salvest made a version of the U.S. flag, the "Stars and Stripes," from 90,000 cigarette butts. His works have also incorporated such everyday objects as business cards, spent coffee filters, wine corks, and even nail clippings.

BALLOON BIKINI ■ Two U.S. fashion designers have created a range of clothing—from bikinis to party dresses—made entirely out of balloons. Each outfit designed by Katie Laibstain of Richmond, Virginia, and Steven Jones of Cincinnati, Ohio, contains around 300 twisted balloons and takes an average of ten hours to make. Even though the dresses can be worn only once, some of the designs have sold for $2,000.

COFFEE STAINS ■ Sunshine Plata of Manila, Philippines, paints with coffee grounds, creating lifelike pictures that look like brown watercolors—but, of course, their smell reveals their true nature.

PATERNAL POT ■ John Lowndes of Pembrokeshire, Wales, missed his daily pot of tea with his father so much that when dad Ian died, John had his ashes made into a teapot. Potter Neil Richardson mixed Ian's ashes straight into the clay so that the teapot was safe to use.

Rubber Robes

Artist Susie MacMurray from Manchester, England, stitched 1,400 rubber gloves together in a flamboyant long-sleeved dress design. Her other rubber glove designs include a strapless ball gown and a wedding dress made from rubber gloves and balloons woven into a mesh foundation.

BOTTLE LAMPS ■ In Kuala Lumpur in May 2008, Lisa Foo and Su Sim from Selangor, Malaysia, exhibited beautiful lamps in the shape of sea creatures and marine organisms—all made from recycled plastic water bottles.

KING KURTA ■ Craftsmen in Pakistan have made a *kurta*—a form of long shirt—large enough to be worn by somebody 175 ft (53.3 m) tall. The garment measures 101 ft (31 m) in length, which is 30 times larger than the average *kurta*, weighs an incredible 1,765 lb (800 kg) and took a team of 50 tailors 30 days to put together.

PIANO-PLAYING FLY ■ Belgian photographer Nicholas Hendrickx has been creating a buzz in the art world by taking quirky pictures of flies. Using his bedroom as his studio, Hendrickx employs miniature props to photograph flies apparently playing the piano, the guitar, skateboarding, cycling, flying a kite, or relaxing on the beach. His art requires great patience, as he mainly uses living insects.

INFLATABLE ANIMALS ■ In 2008, street artist Joshua Allen Harris made sculptures of animals—including bears, seals, and giraffes—from discarded plastic bags and then tied them to ventilation grates above New York City subway lines so that whenever a train rushed through underneath, the surge of air caused the animal to jump up and spring to life.

LIFELIKE ANIMALS ■ Thanks to Joe Wertheimer, people can enjoy the beauty of wild animals on their land without any of the upkeep. The Californian sculptor designs magnificent lifesize animals that, from a distance, are indistinguishable from the real thing. He has carved 18 African animals for a hotel in South Africa and four grazing sheep and a Texas longhorn bull for a client in Malibu.

HIGHWAY DEBRIS ■ To highlight the dangers of road debris, artist Ken Andexler built a sculpture 8 ft (2.4 m) high from 350 discarded items he found along a one-mile stretch of road in Naples, Florida. He included two baking pans, a diver's fin, tennis balls, a wrench, a paintbrush, rusted springs, and various items of scrap metal. The centerpiece was a sign spelling out "Lost and Found" in 176 cigarette butts.